The African Spurred Tortoise
Geochelone sulcata in Captivity

(Professional Breeders Series)

**BY RUSS GURLEY
DIRECTOR, TURTLE AND T
PRESERVATION GROUP**

© 2002 by Taxon Media Publishing, ECO Publishing, and Edition Chimaira, with the Turtle and Tortoise Preservation Group (http://www.ttpg.org/)

**Copies available from
Taxon Media Distributors
P.O. Box 192
403 Parkway Ave. N.
Lanesboro, MN 55949
orders@taxonmedia.com**

ISBN   1-885209-25-8 (U.S., Paperback)

1-885209-26-6 (U.S., Digital Book on CD-Rom)

3-930612-70-4 (Germany, Paperback)

All photos by the author unless otherwise acknowledged.

Front Cover: A young African Spurred Tortoise, Geochelone sulcata, *explores his outdoor environment. Photo by Rusty Mills.*
Back Cover: A group of large Adrican Spurred Tortoises enjoying a meal. Photo by Rusty Mills.

For Fionnuala and little Cait

It is exciting for me when a project becomes complex and convoluted and a variety of friends and colleagues become involved. Several good friends have helped me during the completion of this book.

I would like to thank Rusty Mills for access to his herd of African Spurred Tortoises and for his eagerness to help with this project. His comments and photos have helped me present the lives of both small and large African Spurred Tortoises in captivity.

A special thanks to Jean Kim of Arizona and Adam Stout of Florida. Their offer to provide insights into the lives of African Spurred Tortoises in their respective areas will hopefully help beginning keepers in these environments.

My friend Bill Love provided some beautiful and creative photos for which he is so widely known. His professionalism and enthusiasm were refreshing. Jim Pether provided some great photos of *G. sulcata* in their native habitat and provided some observations of these tortoises in the wild. Sadly, in many areas the African Spurred Tortoises have disappeared or are disappearing.

I would also like to thank Eric Thiss of Zoo Book Sales and Dan Beaver of Taxon Media. Without their support and prodding, this book would probably not exist.

INTRODUCTION

The Turtle and Tortoise Preservation Group was established in 1996 to help promote both the protection of wild chelonians and the production of the world's captive turtles and tortoises. With the help of some of the best keepers and breeders in the United States., we have been able to establish a captive group of turtles and tortoises that we are proud to manage. During the early days of the TTPG, *Geochelone sulcata*, the African Spurred Tortoise, was being imported in relatively large numbers and we were fortunate enough to work with these great animals. The African Spurred Tortoise *Geochelone sulcata* in Captivity is the presentation of our work in written form.

When I was approached to produce this book, I knew part of what I wanted to present. We believe that there is an often overlooked moral responsibility when learning about captive reptiles to expand not only one's knowledge and skills but also to create an enhanced life for one's animals. I have seen some collections of captive animals that are still kept in antiquated, "ease

of maintenance" conditions. These animals sit daily in their tubs or cramped cages, waiting for a mouse, or a hunk of lettuce, living in shadow in a sweater box rack. In other cases, some keepers inspire us with large enclosures planted with orchids and bromeliads and sporting high-tech misting systems. Imagine a tortoise living its life in a large vivarium full of cork bark, palm fronds, live plants, clean water, and stimulation. Setting up the enclosure can be quite enjoyable. The search for plants that are native to an animal's habitat and finding the right sand and the special rock can be exciting. Designing and building an environment that stimulates and inspires both the viewer and the animals within can become a mission. We have a choice.

Captive tortoises are worthy of this type of fervor. After all, these ancient creatures are attached to their environment deeply. They have a focus in their eyes and they are led by a finely tuned sense of smell. They search their habitat, dipping their noses into the soil, rubbing their bodies against objects, and exploring the other inhabitants of their environment.

The African Spurred Tortoise is at something of a crossroads in captivity these days. As a species, it is catching grief from a variety of fronts. Unfortunately, the reputation of sulcatas is even being damaged by reptile enthusiasts who have self-righteously taken it upon themselves to impose their ideas and lack of understanding onto keepers desiring to work responsibly with these large reptiles.

Sulcata tortoises can inspire individual keepers and entire families. By keeping them properly, children and adults learn respect for a living animal and its needs. Daily routines spring up around this new and exotic pet that instill thoughtfulness and responsibility. With the proliferation of forums and chat rooms on the Internet, there has also been a proliferation of care information that is shared, often as gospel. Unfortunately, following some of this information may not be appropriate for many captive situations for sulcata tortoises. There are keepers offering conflicting information and care sheets exist that are not only inconsistent, but even detrimental to the livelihood of these wonderful tortoises.

More and more shows and expos are popping up all over the country. Baby African Spurred Tortoises are available in increasing numbers. Unfortunately, many sellers don't have time to spend with the buyer, and they desire to quickly move on to the next sale. Also, many people who sell these little tortoises don't know precisely how to care for them, offering a general overview of what they know about the care of <u>any</u> baby tortoise.

From a small tan hatchling with wide, alert eyes and a ravenous appetite, these wonderful tortoises quickly (in tortoise terms) can become backyard giants. They grow very large and incredibly heavy with needs that outweigh many keepers' expectations and abilities.

We hope that you find this book helpful whether you are caring for a single hatchling *G. sulcata* or managing a large group of lawn-mowing giants.

RUSS GURLEY
Director
Turtle and Tortoise Preservation Group

Contents

Chapter ONE: THE AFRICAN SPURRED TORTOISE IN NATURE

The African Spurred Tortoise, *Geochelone sulcata*, is the world's third largest tortoise, only smaller than the giant island-dwelling Galapagos and Aldabra tortoises. In nature, this tortoise is found living in a large swath across North-Central Africa south of the Sahara Desert from Mauritania to Ethiopia.

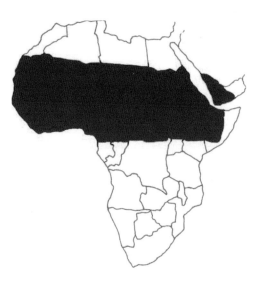

This area of Africa is hot and dry. Temperatures range from the 60s F in the coldest part of winter (June to August in this part

Former Geochelone sulcata *habitat between Dakar and Saint-Louis, Senegal. Sadly, African Spurred Tortoises are no longer found here due to human interference, habitat destruction, and loss of food from the introduction of goats. Photo by Jim Pether.*

A large sulcata feeding at night to avoid the extreme heat of a summer day. Photo by Rusty Mills.

of the world) to well over 100° F (38° C) during the summer. Incredibly, this area receives very little rainfall with some areas receiving no rain for several years at a time (Kaplan, 1996).

African Spurred Tortoises are diggers. In fact, they are one of only a few tortoises that burrow extensively in nature. As adults, these giants dig deep tunnels in which to spend the long dry season and to escape the intense heat of the African sun. In addition to some protection from heat and predators, the burrows provide a humid area for absorption of small amounts of moisture as the hot days are exchanged for cooler nights. It is reported that in many areas African Spurred Tortoises are active at dusk and dawn feeding before the heat hits (Ernst and Barbour, 1989). Captive observations at the Turtle and Tortoise Preservation Group show this behavior to be not uncommon.

African Spurred Tortoises feed on grasses, shrubs, and succulent plants in their natural habitat. Most of the moisture they need is obtained from these plants. Their growth in nature is slow and it may take up to 24 years for African Spurred Tortoises to reach maturity in the wild (Lambert, 1993). This is due largely to their life in an environment that is hospitable for only about four months of the year and with eight months of extreme heat and aridity and little vegetation available.

Chapter TWO: ANATOMY

Their harsh natural environment has produced in sulcatas an animal that is strong, resilient, and adaptable. Adult African Spurred Tortoises are extremely powerful and heavy with broad, flattened carapaces. They have dry, thick, scaly skin that helps to prevent water loss in their arid homes. These tortoises have the sturdy, broad elephantine feet typical of land tortoises. Both males and females have spurs on the back legs on each side of the tail. These spurs give this species its common name. Males of this awesome tortoise grow up to 30" straight line shell length and commonly reach weights of over 120 pounds. The largest *G. sulcata* recorded was a very large male that was 42" and weighed over 225 pounds (Flower, 1928). Females are typically smaller, reaching only 20 to 24" and weighing from 65 to 75 pounds.

THE SHELL

Sulcatas are solidly built with a thick, strong shell. They range in color from sandy tan to dark brown in color. The carapace is flattened, with grooved seams (sulcata means grooved),

This adult male sulcata sports the enlarged gulars used for combat. Photo by Rusty Mills.

and unlike other tortoises, they are nearly square when viewed from above. The plastron features gular projections that are forked. These large, solid gulars are elongated in the males and are used by them for slamming into other male sulcatas and for pushing against other tortoises and obstacles in captivity.

Occasionally, large sulcatas will have a hole in the back marginal scutes. This hole was used for tethering wild-caught specimens to a tree or stake before they were sold and exported.

African Spurred Tortoises have large heads and powerful jaws. Photo by Rusty Mills.

THE HEAD

The sulcata's head is large and solid. Its eyes are inquisitive, with an unyielding focus, especially if food is nearby. The nasal openings of a healthy African Spurred Tortoise are clear and dry, symbolic of its desert-dwelling life. Its strong jaws are notched above for chopping through coarse vegetable matter and its tongue is large, fleshy, and pink.

THE LEGS

African Spurred Tortoises have powerful, muscular legs covered with dry, scaly skin. These scales are oversized and thick-

The spurs which can be easily seen in larger sulcatas give this African species its common name. Photo by Rusty Mills.

ened, including the two or three large spurs that give this tortoise its common name.

THE TAIL
Sulcata tails are relatively short in both sexes, but an adult female's tail is significantly shorter than that of the male.

ABNORMALITIES

PYRAMIDING
Pyramiding is a condition where a tortoise shows abnormal growth on its carapace, making it look bumpy. This is caused when a tortoise eats a diet that is too high in protein and low in calcium. It is most often seen in captive sulcatas when they are fed solely on commercial foods or when cat food or dog food is added to their diet.

Pyramiding in a three-year old captive-raised *Geochelone sulcata*.

IRREGULAR SCUTES
Occasionally, young sulcatas are seen with irregular scutes. There are reports of this condition occasionally occurring in nature, but typically these irregular scutes are caused when an egg

The irregular scutes seen in this young sulcata tortoise are most likely a sign of high incubation temperatures. Photo by Rusty Mills.

has been incubated too hot either accidentally or by a breeder trying to rush the incubation time.

SOFT SHELL

Soft shell is a severe malady in tortoises that arises from lack of direct sunlight, lack of dietary calcium, or excessive phosphorus in the diet. Soft shell develops when a tortoise's blood stream shaves calcium from its bones and its shell to meet the calcium needs of the muscular and other body systems, leaving the tortoise's shell soft and pliable. This condition can be corrected by the addition of calcium and vitamin supplements onto the afflicted tortoise's food and by the addition of plenty of natural sunlight which allows the tortoise's body to use this calcium properly.

Chapter THREE:
CHOOSING A TORTOISE

If you are thinking about getting an African Spurred Tortoise, there are several things to consider . . .

Spurred Tortoises get very large and require a lot of space and they should be kept outside as much as possible.

Spurred Tortoises need to be kept hot and dry. If they get too damp and cold, they can develop serious medical problems that will probably require a veterinarian's care.

This small African Spurred Tortoise is alert and interested in his grassy surroundings.

These tortoises do not hibernate so they must be housed indoors or in a warm building during the winter in a temperate environment.

Spurred Tortoises are very strong and spend a great deal of their time digging and pushing against objects. The can do damage to fences, landscaping, and other property.

Spurred Tortoises typically do not mix well with dogs and other tortoises. As male African Spurred Tortoises approach breeding size they may become aggressive, ramming other tortoises, pets, and even people. Recently, at a well-known tortoise breeder's facilities, a large male sulcata rammed, intimidated, and killed a Galapagos Tortoise that was nearly twice its height and weight.

Well cared for African Spurred Tortoises can live for many years, so they will require a long-term obligation.

If you weigh all of these considerations and are willing to make the commitment, then a Spurred Tortoise may be right for you.

Finding a Tortoise

Once you have decided to get a sulcata tortoise and after you have read this book, the search begins . . .

PET & SPECIALTY STORES

As interest grows, more and more pet stores are offering tortoises for sale. Not only are they offering tortoises for pets, but they are exhibiting healthy animals in proper and inspiring setups. Many are offering correct advice and stocking the best equipment and supplies for their customers. In the past, pet stores rarely established proper enclosures to keep tortoises long-term. Heating and diet were inappropriate and specimens were often in poor health and species from all over the world were mixed together in a single, large cage. As imported specimens made up most of the tortoises for sale in the shops, most were traumatized and parasitized. Now, with the increased emphasis on the true needs of tortoises, shops are installing larger enclosures with basking spots and they are offering a healthy diet. Many are even offering veterinary services to care for tortoises before or during sales times.

This group of two week-old G. sulcata *tortoises are offered heat from above and below as they rest before being moved to their first enclosures.*

Though many continue to get a bad rap, these shops are literally the front line in the crusade to educate the general public about tortoises. As the first stop for most people searching for a pet tortoise, pet shops have the

This three-week old African Spurred Tortoise looks healthy and alert.

unique ability to inspire a beginning tortoise keeper's first creative ideas and to offer proper procedures for setting up and caring for animals.

Choosing a Specific Tortoise

When you discover a tortoise that you are interested in purchasing, begin by checking out the tortoise's enclosure. Check the substrate. It should be clean and tortoises should not be crowded. If tortoises from different parts of the world are kept together, especially in crowded conditions, we suggest you don't buy any.

Ask about the tortoise that has caught your eye. Was it bred by the person you are talking to? Was it bred locally? What's it been through over the last few days? Was it purchased from a breeder? Was it purchased from a dealer? Was it shipped? If the salesperson gets irritated, assure them that you are not trying to track down their sources and that you are just trying to see what this tortoise has been through prior to your purchase.

• Pick up the tortoise. It should be alert, active, and heavy.

- Check its strength. It should push off of your fingers with force.

- Check its uniformity. The shape of the scutes should not be irregular and there should be no noticeable bumps, lumps, or asymmetry to its body. The profile should also be symmetrical.

- Check its eyes. They should not be puffy and should be clear, mucus-free, and alert.

- Check its nostrils. The nostrils should be open and free from any bubbles or discharge.

- Check its mouth. The mouth should be free from injuries, irregularities, or lumps.

- Check its vent. Its cloacal opening and tail should be free of any discharge or lumps.

Ask about any guarantee the seller might offer. Is this guarantee offered in writing? Remember, your choice is often final and you will have no possibility of a refund. In fairness, the seller can't know your facilities or the care you will offer and so can only guarantee the tortoise's current health.

SHOWS AND EXPOS

In recent years, reptile shows and expos have become very popular. In the last few years there has been an increase in the number of captive-produced turtles and tortoises at these shows. Typically the specimens offered at these shows are healthy, feeding well, and excellent specimens to begin a tortoise-keeping hobby or to add to an existing collection. At these shows you get the rare opportunity to hand pick the animal you want to purchase. When having a tortoise shipped to you, there is always the risk of receiving a tortoise that is picked by someone who may not have your best interest at heart. Add to the savings of not having to pay shipping and the lack of stress placed on the animal from shipping and the shows and expos are often an excellent opportunity to get a really nice tortoise.

The top U.S. shows include the National Reptile Breeders Expo in Florida, the N.A.R.B.C. shows in Chicago and Philadelphia, the IRBA shows on the west coast, the ETHS Conference and Expo in

Houston, and the Texas Reptile Expos. There are dozens of other great local shows throughout the country. These shows can be located on the Internet, through local herpetological societies, and they are advertised in reptile magazines and journals. It is well worth the effort to track them down.

TORTOISE BREEDERS

Some keepers are fortunate to have a local tortoise breeder near their home. Often, these breeders will welcome visitors (potential customers) to their facilities. In this situation, you get to see the breeder's facilities and see his or her animals. You might learn some of their tricks, glean some experience and helpful hints from them, and often gain a new friend or colleague with which to share ideas and offspring. You can find these breeders through a local herp society, a reptile keeper at the local zoo, ads in a reptile magazine, or on the Internet.

An assortment of African Spurred Tortoises from one-week old to a very large adult. Photo by Rusty Mills.

THE INTERNET

The Internet has very quickly developed into the largest source of live animals ever imagined. There are several extensive websites that offer classified ad sections where you can order animals and plants as well as heat lamps, UV bulbs, cages, vitamins, food, and more. There have been occasional problems with unscrupulous, faceless dealers. You don't get to see the facilities and many of these Internet dealers are simply buying and reselling animals. Some don't disclose to beginners that an animal is captive-produced or wild-caught, or even worse lie and say that it is when it isn't. There are also concerns about shipping, even with overnight delivery services.

There are Styrofoam-lined boxes, disposable heat packs, and most boxes can travel across the country in a day without a problem. However, we have received boxes from supposedly professional dealers that had a half dozen animals stuffed into a pillowcase and placed into an empty box. No packing material, no Styrofoam liner, and a resulting disastrous event.

If you are careful and inquisitive, these Internet dealers can be a good source for tortoises. When contacting people selling tortoises, ask plenty of questions. These people want to sell you a live tortoise (or tortoises) and keep you as a future customer so they should be willing to spend a little extra time with you. Make sure they are charging a fair price by looking around at what these animals typically sell for in other ads and from other sources such as pet stores, breeders, and dealer price lists. Do your homework. Most sellers will be willing to send you photos of the specific animal in which you are interested. Find out about their packing and shipping techniques. Make sure they sound logical and safe for the animal. If the seller is rude or unwilling to answer your questions, move on and count your blessings. Typically, these deals end up being the ones you regret.

There is some confusion about which shipping companies will ship turtles and tortoises. Currently, it depends on the company, where you live, and how knowledgeable the individual who helps you is. Check around locally with carriers offering overnight service. As an individual, the airline freight companies will not be able to work with you. Recent events have made shipping by air freight nearly impossible except for the large dealers that have been willing to jump through the required "hoops". Your best bet is the big companies offering overnight shipping such as Airborne Express, Federal Express, and UPS.

UNITED STATES POSTAL SERVICE
USPS regulation: United States Postal Service, Hazardous, Restricted, and Perishable Material, Publication 52, 1999

525.3 Reptiles – All snakes, turtles, and poisonous reptiles are nonmailable.

"Turtles are the only living members of the subclass Anapsida, which is characterized by a primitive skull with a solid cranium and no temporal openings (anapsid). These shelled reptiles constitute the order Testudines. All living shelled reptiles are turtles, but the terms tortoise and terrapin have also been applied, and these have different meanings in various parts of the world. Tortoise is best applied to terrestrial turtles. Terrapin is usually applied to edible, more or less aquatic, hard-shelled turtles."

> *Turtles of the World*
>
> C. H. Ernst, R.G.M. Altenburg, and R.W. Barbour

Quarantine

Even with a captive-hatched sulcata we suggest a quarantine period of 30 to 45 days before you add it to your exist-

---

SHIPPING TORTOISES

Place the animal carefully into a pillow case or cloth bag. (Occasionally, we place smaller tortoises into a small cardboard box, similar in size to a shoe box that has been perforated with lots of holes and stuffed full of dry or lightly dampened sphagnum moss.) Place the animals so that they are fairly tightly packed inside. This prevents them from banging their legs around or injuring their head or neck when the box is moved around.

Place the bag or small box into a larger, Styrofoam-lined cardboard shipping box. (These boxes are available on the Internet or through your local pet store as they are used to transport tropical fish. They usually cost from $8.00 to $10.00 each.)

Fill in around the pillow case or small box with packing material such as biodegradable "peanuts" or wadded up newspaper. Again, make sure that the animals cannot bang around inside the box. They don't need to crawl or stretch out as they travel. If they can breathe easily and not get injured when the box is bounced around, they will be safest.

---

ing collection. Many new keepers will even choose to have a fecal sample checked by a local veterinarian just to be safe.

TTPG Rule: Don't mix species together. We feel that this is very important on many different levels. The requirements of other species of tortoises such as Red-footed Tortoises and Yellow-footed Tortoises are radically different than those of your Spurred Tortoise. Red-footed Tortoises and Yellow-footed Tortoises like it hot and humid. Central Asian (Russian) Tortoises require similar captive conditions to African Spurred Tortoises but are not a good species to mix with African species. Leopard Tortoises like it hot and dry and get quite large. Many keepers mix Spurred Tortoises and Leopard Tortoises. We know of cases where aggressive Spurred Tortoises have rammed and injured Leopard Tortoises. Leopard Tortoises are typically shy and sensitive and will stress out very quickly if shoved and prodded by the incessant attacks of even much smaller sulcatas. In addition, it is felt by most keepers that bacteria, viruses, and parasites can be passed from one tortoise species to another and the results may be more harmful than a simple cross-contamination.

SHIPPING TORTOISES (CONT.)

Tape the box shut securely with strapping tape.

During hot months, we perforate each side of the outer box and Styrofoam liner with six to eight holes about the diameter of a pencil. Make sure the holes are in the outer cardboard box and the inner Styrofoam liner. During cooler months or when traveling during a cold night, we only add two or three perforations in each side. Most reptile shippers feel that the small openings around the flaps of the box, Styrofoam lid, etc. offer enough air in and out during the relatively short travel time.

Label the box LIVE HARMLESS REPTILES or LIVE TORTOISES and PERISHABLE and note which end is up on the top and sides of the box. (We often add PLEASE AVOID EXTREME HEAT or PLEASE AVOID EXTREME COLD as well.)

Chapter FOUR: INTERVIEWS

Keepers are successfully raising and breeding African Spurred Tortoises in a variety of environments around the world. Many of them are successful even in oddly non-sulcata-friendly conditions. We would like to share tips and helpful hints from these three sulcata keepers.

Rusty Mills, Oklahoma

"Keeping African Spurred Tortoises in Oklahoma has been lots of fun. They are very interactive and I spend most afternoons and weekends with them. Our summers are typically very hot and dry which is the ideal environment for them. I keep a group in my modified back yard. It took lots of time and some extra expense to get the yard ready for them. I took  down my chain link fence and put up a privacy fence and had two small buildings put up at the back. One is for keeping babies and young sulcatas and supplies and the other is for keeping the large adult tortoises inside during the winter. It is also used as a shelter in the warmer months and as a nighttime sleeping enclosure. I believe by providing them with this "house" it discourages them from digging tunnels my yard. I have never had any of the sulcatas I have kept attempt to dig tunnels as long as they are provided with some sort of house. Two or three times a week, I get leftover vegetables and fruit from a local farmers market. From this the tortoises receive a large variety of over twenty different greens, vegetables, spineless cactus, and fruits. I also offer them treats of pumpkins after Halloween, over-ripe melons, and whatever special items the vendors have for me that week.

A large sulcata roams a snow-covered enclosure on a bright sunny winter day. Photo by Rusty Mills.

My sulcata usually begin breeding early in the summer as it starts to warm up. I usually get my first clutch of eggs in October. The second clutch is usually exactly thirty days later in November and I get a third clutch in December. Every once in a while, I will have a female lay eggs in January or Feburary (after they've been moved to their indoor winter quarters). Laying eggs this late into the colder months of the the year can be problematic, so I have modified my barn to allow for the females to lay their eggs in a recessed floor area filled with sand and soil. There is also a small doorway going into this area which does not allow the larger males into the laying area. This prevents them from disturbing the females as they attempt to deposit their eggs. The indoor laying area is not always used by the females and if they start pacing and begin showing signs of stress, I give them an injection of oxytocin which initiates the laying of the eggs within 4-6 hours. I have to be sure to be there to catch the eggs as the female will usually just lay them on the surface of the enclosure.

Interestingly, after laying the eggs, she will continue to dig nests and pace the enclosure for a few days. This is probably a result of the unnatural conditions in which she laid her eggs. I don't recommend getting eggs this way, but rather than lose the female from egg-binding, I have chosen to use the oxytocin. You should find a local vet that is able to organize this procedure for you.

Baby sulcatas also do very well in our hot and dry summers. I have constructed small outdoor enclosures in a variety of shapes and sizes from landscape posts that are held in place with metal stakes. I add ornamental grasses such as Pampas Grass and Zebra Grass and often keep piles of drift wood inside to give the babies some shade and a feeling of security. They seem to love to pick at the grass and weeds in their pen all day.

We have two main enemies in Oklahoma and Texas. One is predators and the other is the cold. There are usually quite a few predators of baby tortoises in our area. Even in the larger cities, there are usually raccoons, opossums, and even neighborhood cats that want to come and make a meal of our baby tortoises. To be safe, I bring some of the smaller tortoises into one of our buildings during the night. Others are offered pens with secure tops made of wood and chicken wire or welded wire. Once the tortoises reach 4-5 inches, they seem to be less likely to be harassed by predators. Unlike fellow keepers in Texas and other areas of the south, we don't have to worry about fire ants. Fire ants are becoming a real problem in some areas and can kill tortoises and box turtles very quickly.

We have cold winters and all of the tortoises must come inside during this time. We maintain the temperature inside this building in the 70° to 80° F range, but occasional nighttime lows reach the 55° to 60° F range. As long as they get a warm-up during the day (80° F), we have experienced no problems. On a cold but sunny day, I will occasionally let the larger tortoises outside. This is when I like to feed them because 100 lbs. of assorted veggies can get really messy on the inside. The tortoises are fed inside their winter buildings smaller amounts about

This large African Spurred Tortoise is enjoying a snack of carrots. Photo by Rusty Mills.

once a week. They seem to not mind the rest and emerge in the spring ready to eat, breed, and reproduce."

Jean Kim, Arizona

"Obviously, southern Arizona is the ideal place to keep and breed African Spurred Tortoises. Our environment very closely matches their natural habitat. Interestingly, one of the problems we deal with is the extreme heat of summer. We must be careful to offer our tortoises a shady place to keep out of the hottest afternoons. We use dog houses and wooden structures to provide plenty of shade. Some of our tortoises will dig burrows, but we try to minimize this digging by filling in the burrows with large stones to dissuade them from digging them too deep. This is mainly because we don't want them digging up our yard and also because we would like to be able to move them around and check on them each day. If they are down inside a burrow for a few days to a week, we are not sure how they are doing.

During our coldest winter nights, we offer the tortoises a little extra heat inside their dog houses in the form of a 100 watt bulb in a clip-on lamp attached to the inside of the roof of the dog house. This single bulb keeps the temperature up around 60° to 65° F which is our goal.

We offer all of our African Spurred Tortoises lots of local grass and weeds to insure that they have a natural, healthy diet. We divide our tortoise enclosure into quarters. We keep 1/4 of this pen without any tortoises inside. We let the grass in this yard grow freely for several months. Then, we move tortoises into this area and let another 1/4 of the yard grow back. This rotation prevents any of the areas from getting too over grazed which can cause them to turn into a barren and sometimes muddy mess. In addition to grasses, we feed a lot of spineless Opuntia (Prickly Pear Cactus) pads, cactus fruit, and other desert plants. These are high in calcium and fiber and low in protein which is perfect for these tortoises."

Adam Stout, Florida

"We have lots of bright sunshine in Florida. This is obviously great for our African Spurred Tortoises. You would think that the humidity is too high here for them, but we have kept them for almost ten years and have seen no ill effects. We have to be careful during our rainy season. We let the tortoises stay inside a small barn during very wet weather and we have landscaped so there is no standing water. Also, their outdoor building is raised on blocks so the water does not soak into the flooring of the building.

The tortoises seem to love our sandy soil here. They dig a lot and seem to enjoy digging in the sand, even with their noses. Egg-

A large African Spurred Tortoise rests at the entrance of its burrow in a private collection in Florida. Photo by Bill Love.

laying is also an easy task for our females and we find it very easy to dig up the eggs when we choose to incubate them indoors. Occasionally we will let the eggs incubate in the ground. We have had great success with this when the nest is protected by a large screen box with weights on top to keep the raccoons out. If you do not protect the nest, the eggs will get eaten - guaranteed!

We feed our sulcatas lots of grasses, fresh hay, banana leaves, and flowers from the yard. The goal is to keep fiber content high and protein low. We have never used a commercial tortoise diet. Our tortoises are especially fond of large flowers. Though we have a lot of exotic fruit available here, we feed them only small amounts about once a week.

Our most sincere hint: Never mix species together. You are asking for trouble if your tortoise collection grows and you begin putting species together. It is unnatural and problems will occur.

We also suggest that you find a good veterinarian before you have any problems. Keep the phone number by the phone just like you would for the police, fire department, and other important numbers."

Chapter FIVE: INDOOR ENCLOSURES

Raising a sulcata tortoise indoors is tricky. Though they have proven to be extremely hardy in a variety of environments, they have a very close relationship with the sun and the heat and UV rays that it provides. If a keeper is diligent, he or she can provide the nutritional supplements and heat that this species requires in an indoor situation. One should however, let these tortoises live outside whenever possible. We have found the best indoor enclosures for African Spurred Tortoises to be glass terrariums, tubs, and stock tanks.

SMALL TORTOISES
GLASS TERRARIUMS

The first enclosure for a small tortoise can be a terrarium in the 10 to 20 gallon range. We have found 20-gallon long aquariums to be ideal. The length of these aquariums (30" x 12" x 12") gives you a good space to establish a temperature gradient within the enclosure. By placing a clamp type fixture with a 75-watt bulb over one end, the keeper can establish the required 90° to 95°

This African Spurred Tortoise enclosure was created using a 20-gallon long aquarium. It features a shelter made from bricks (resting solidly on the bottom) and a flat piece of slate. The substrate is rabbit pellets. A clip fixture with a 75 watt incandescent bulb is attached over the "hot" end and a fluorescent fixture with UVB-emitting bulbs is mounted overhead.

F (32° to 35° C) basking spot that is essential for growing African Spurred Tortoises. The length of the long enclosure typically allows the other end to stay in the 80° to 85° F (27° to 29° C)

This African Spurred Tortoise enclosure was made from a 40-gallon breeder aquarium with a ceramic shelter and clumps of live plants for shade and exercise. A fluorescent fixture and an incandescent spot light provide both UVB and heat.

range. Be careful. Don't put these glass enclosures outside in the sun. Glass aquariums can heat up very quickly and though heat-lovers, these little tortoises can dehydrate and die quickly if they are not given access to some shade via a shelter.

There is no need for a top to this enclosure unless you need it to support heat lamps or light fixtures or if you have small children or pets that will be likely to get into the enclosure.

SUBSTRATE

There are almost as many ideas about the proper substrate for small tortoises as there are tortoise keepers. Many breeders suggest using paper towel as it is easy to clean and is inexpensive. When the towel gets soiled, it can be easily removed and replaced with new.

Rabbit pellets are a good substrate because they are made from compressed alfalfa hay. If the small tortoise is a sloppy eater, and gets some chunks of the rabbit pellets as it feeds, they simply add to its meal.

A sand and peat mixture is a natural substrate and supports the naturalistic captive environment ideal that we promote. With the addition of rocks, wood, and plants (protected from the voracious tortoises by rock barriers or large clay pots) one can design an interesting and exciting tortoise enclosure. Some keepers are concerned about young tortoises accidentally ingesting sand as they eat. We feed our tortoises on small trays or plates so there is

---

little access to the substrate while they are eating. Over the years, we have never lost a tortoise to sand impaction.

HEAT AND LIGHTING

The hobby of keeping turtles and tortoises has grown dramatically in the last five years. With this growth has been an associated proliferation of products related to their care. Many of these products are misleading for new keepers. Among the most confusing of these products are the lighting and heating accessories.

HEAT

For heat, we suggest a clip lamp fixture and an incandescent bulb in the 75 to 100 watt range. These bulbs provide heat in a "basking spot" area which is important to most tortoise species. As mentioned above, high heat and aridity with a temperature gradient ranging from 80° F (27° C) to 95° F (35° C) is necessary to keep these tortoises healthy. We mount the fixture about 12" above the substrate to provide a hot spot for the tortoises. During the winter or in cooler rooms, we add a heating pad on the low setting underneath the "hot" end of their vivarium for a little added heat.

LIGHTING AND NUTRITION

Sun-loving, diurnal species such as the African Spurred Tortoise require vitamin D3 for the metabolism of calcium in their bodies. They produce this vitamin D3 by absorbing UV rays from the sun. Vitamin D3 is not found in plant material, so vitamin supplements containing D3 can be added to the diet which will essentially simulate this process. For those species tied closely to the sun, there is no question that the addition of natural sunlight is beneficial even with the proper use of dietary supplements.

Captive tortoises not exposed to natural sunlight and those not exposed to an artificial source of high-quality UVB emissions run a very real risk of developing metabolic bone disease (MBD). MBD is a dangerous condition that occurs most commonly in young tortoises that are growing quickly and in egg-laying females. This condition leaves tortoises with soft, pliable shells and growth deformities that are not only abnormal, but also life threatening. In fact, it is reported that MBD is the most common cause of death in many types of young, captive reptiles (Highfield, 2002).

There are dozens of fluorescent and incandescent bulbs on the market and available through pet stores that bill themselves as "full spectrum", "basking lights", "reptile bulbs", etc. However, there are very few that actually emit the UVB rays needed for the proper utilization of calcium by captive reptiles. A few, including Active UV-heat bulb® by T-REX, Zoomed's Reptisun 5.0 ®, Big Apple 7.0 SunBlast® bulbs, and Exo-Terra® 5.0 or 8.0 bulbs have actually proven to effectively boost and restore vitamin D3 levels in reptilian blood and many keepers have reported increased activity and more "natural" behaviors in their captive reptiles. These bulbs work well as long as a few important conditions are observed.

1. These bulbs need to be placed from 12" to 18" above the animals. Further distances greatly reduce their efficiency.

2. The rays emitted from these bulbs must not be obstructed by plastic, plexiglass, or glass. They must be mounted above an open enclosure or must rest on a screen top of some sort.

3. These bulbs need to be replaced at least once each year. (Active UV-heat bulbs® by T-REX reportedly last considerably longer than the others mentioned.) We mark each bulb with a marker noting the date it was installed so we know when to replace it.

We use shop light fixtures or fluorescent aquarium fixtures with two high-quality UVB bulbs (ZOOMED's Reptisun 5.0® bulbs, Big Apple 7.0 Sunblast® bulbs, Exo-Terra® 5.0 or 8.0 bulbs, etc.) and one incandescent fixture with an T-REX Active UV-heat bulb® above all of our indoor turtles and tortoises. We feel that this combination of bulbs puts out a sufficient amount of UVB indoors and they are used alongside the added vitamin and calcium supplementation.

In addition to lighting, many reptile keepers are now experimenting with controlling the calcium needs of their captives through diet rather than access to sunlight. Some believe that when offered in the proper proportions (vitamin D3 along with 2 parts calcium to 1 part phosphorus), dietary supplementation can provide the needs of most diurnal reptiles.

SHELTER / CAGE DECORATIONS

Security and an escape from the heat can be offered by a variety of shelters. Cork bark, drift wood, commercial shelters, and even upside-down shoe boxes with a doorway, make excellent shelters for small tortoises.

MEDIUM TORTOISES
GLASS TERRARIUMS

The enclosure for a medium sulcata can be an aquarium in the 40 to 60 gallon range or a medium tub or stock tank. We have found the shorter and longer aquariums to be ideal. Once again, choose a terrarium that gives you enough space to establish a temperature gradient within the enclosure. Ex: 40 gallon breeder - (48" x 13" x 16") - 58 gallon - (36" x 18" x 21").

This creative indoor environment houses one medium-sized African Spurred Tortoise.

TUBS

A variety of plastic / polyethylene tubs are available to tortoise keepers. We suggest purchasing the largest ones possible for your available space. Watching tortoises from above is an interesting change for most keepers. There is often a feeling of watching them in their world - a natural area far from the hustle and bustle of everyday life.

A variety of tubs are available that make wonderful enclosures for turtles and tortoises.

Our medium tubs are 72" x 36" x 12". Tubs this size are produced by a few different companies and are distributed by specialty pet stores and several herp supply retailers. We have used VISION tubs® and Neodesha Tortoise Tubs®. They are lightweight and easy to move and clean. We have found them both to be excellent enclosures for small and medium tortoises.

STOCK TANKS

In most parts of the country, galvanized metal or plastic stock tanks are available in a variety of shapes and sizes from farm and garden stores. We have used these tanks in indoor and outdoor settings for terrestrial, semi-aquatic, and aquatic species with success. The metal ones are thicker-walled, which makes them somewhat heavier than the other tubs, but they have several advantages including depth (24"), strength and sturdiness, a variety of

This African Spurred Tortoise is enjoying the security of its shelter, a commercial cave made of simulated stone.

sizes and shapes, and a pre-drilled drain hole. Their oval and round shapes sometimes fit easier into a turtle keeper's established space.

SUBSTRATE

A sand and peat mixture is a natural and inexpensive substrate in these larger enclosures. With the addition of rocks, wood, and plants (protected from the voracious tortoises by rock barriers or large clay pots), one can design an interesting and exciting tortoise enclosure.

Rabbit pellets are a good substrate for tortoises in these tubs because they are inexpensive.

HEAT

As mentioned above, high heat and aridity with a temperature gradient is necessary to keep these tortoises healthy. In the medium-sized enclosures we typically use a clip lamp fixture with an incandescent bulb mounted about 12" above the substrate to provide a hot spot for the tortoises. This hot spot is kept at 90° to 95° F (32° to 35° C). During the winter we add an extra heat lamp or place an inexpensive heating pad underneath the tub for a little added heat.

LIGHTING

We use shop light fixtures with high-quality UVB bulbs (ZOOMED's Reptisun 5.0® bulbs, Exo-Terra® 5.0 or 8.0 bulbs, etc.) and a T-REX Active UV® bulb above all of our indoor turtles and tortoises.

SHELTERS

Security and an escape from the heat are offered by a variety of shelters. Cork bark, large pieces of drift wood, and large commercial shelters make excellent safe places for medium-sized tortoises.

LARGE TORTOISES

From the photos and text already encountered here, you will now know that sulcata tortoises get very large. Even though this process takes a relatively long time (5 to 8 years or more in captivity) you must have a plan in place. With some modifications, you will be able to keep your large tortoise well indoors for periods of time. Be aware that if you keep large sulcatas inside, they will require a large tub or stock tank. Many keepers have even used a utility room or a basement. Be aware that these large tortoises will produce a large amount of waste and very soon your house will reek of tortoise feces. Even with diligent daily care the smell will persist. Add to this the fact that indoor sulcatas that roam free will wreck your furniture and terrorize your pets. These are just a couple of reasons why large sulcatas should be outside.

TUBS

If your tortoises are kept for some time indoors, we suggest purchasing the largest tubs possible for your available space.

At the TTPG, our largest tubs are 84" x 48" x 24". Tubs this size are produced by a few different companies and are distributed by several herp supply retailers. We have used large VISION tubs® with success. We have found them to be excellent winter enclosures for several medium tortoises or one large tortoises. These tubs are relatively lightweight and easy to move and clean.

STOCK TANKS

In most parts of the country, galvanized metal or plastic stock tanks are available in a variety of sizes and shapes. They are sturdy and somewhat heavier than the other tubs, but they have several advantages including depth (24"), strength and sturdiness, and a variety of sizes and shapes.

SUBSTRATE

These larger enclosures leave you fewer options for substrate.

Cypress mulch, hardwood mulch, and a sand and peat mixture are all natural substrates that work well for larger sulcatas.

Rabbit pellets are good because they are inexpensive and easy to clean and/or replace.

HEAT

We use a clip lamp fixture mounted above the substrate to provide a hot spot of 95° F (35° C) for even the largest tortoises. Indoors, during the winter, we add a second or third lamp and occasionally a heating pad under their enclosure for a little extra heat.

LIGHTING

We use shop light fixtures with high-quality UVB bulbs and one T-REX Active UV® bulb in a clip fixture above our indoor tortoise enclosures.

SHELTER / CAGE DECORATIONS

Larger tortoises are very destructive when it comes to cage decorations. We have found that adding a few piles of prairie hay or straw into these enclosures gives them a place to feel secure. They often sleep under these piles of hay.

Most sulcata keepers establish indoor winter quarters for large tortoises. These winter quarters can be inside a home or in an outbuilding or greenhouse. These buildings are usually divided into stalls or large stock tanks are set up inside for separating males and for separating smaller and larger specimens. If this system is established, each stall should have a source of heat. In areas with cold winters, keepers will often add a gas or electric heater. Be sure to keep this heater raised off the floor or have it mounted securely so tortoises can't tip it over and start a fire. Heat lamps can be added for extra heat as well. These lamps can be placed on timers for the addition of daytime heat. Fiberglass furrowing pads ("pig blankets") can also be added for extra heat from beneath.

Chapter SIX: OUTDOOR ENCLOSURES

The benefits of natural sunlight and outdoor heat for a sun-loving tortoise from arid Africa are obvious. Also, the large size attained by *G. sulcata* makes it a prime candidate for outdoor enclosures.

SMALL TORTOISES

Even small (2-6") African Spurred Tortoises should be offered outdoor enclosures. They can be kept quite easily in tubs and tanks or in pens fashioned from posts or railroad ties. Smaller enclosures can be used, but al-

A beautiful outdoor enclosure for small to medium tortoises. Photo by Rusty Mills.

ways offer your tortoises as much space as possible, especially outdoors. Substrate can be sand or a sand-peat mixture or a pesticide- and herbicide-free patch of lawn. Add some nice pieces of cork bark, driftwood, and plenty of vegetation such as ornamental grasses and piles of leaves to add a feeling of security and to offer the little tortoises some shade. You can also add some shade over the top of part of their enclosure

A very nice outdoor enclosure for small tortoises. The back ledge and clumps of ornamental grasses provide plenty of shade for the small tortoises.

with a nearby tree or "roof" made of a wooden plank or piece of shade cloth.

In some areas, it is imperative that the top of the enclosure is securely covered to keep predators out. We have used tops made from a wooden frame with strong hardware cloth attached. This secure top will keep predators out and let UV rays through. Don't use window screening, as it will typically not deter predators. Predators of smaller tortoises can include raccoons, opossums, large birds, dogs and cats, foxes, coyotes, and even ants in some areas.

Nowadays many keepers have to add locks to their outdoor tortoise enclosures. Theft by humans is becoming more and more common as people discover the value of these tortoises or are attracted by their awesome size.

MEDIUM TORTOISES

Outdoors, medium-sized (8-12") sulcatas can live in similar, only larger pens or enclosures.

Sulcatas do very well in a pen on the ground. We stack railroad ties or landscape posts into a variety of sizes and shapes. You will need to drive metal or wooden stakes to reinforce the pen, even for medium tortoises. They are so strong! Add a shelter or

---

This medium African Spurred Tortoise is resting on the grassy lawn of its outdoor enclosure. Photo by Rusty Mills.

two inside. These shelters can be small doghouses, homemade structures, or clumps of ornamental grasses. Shrubs and small trees will add to the beauty of any outdoor sulcata enclosure.

LARGE TORTOISES

Large African Spurred Tortoises will require big, secure outdoor enclosures or an entire back yard in which to roam. A sturdy fence is a must and will probably need to be reinforced with concrete blocks or staked railroad ties as large sulcatas tend to "test" fences by pushing and digging.

If their enclosure is fenced, a stockade or privacy fence is much better than a chain link fence because without a visual barrier the tortoise will usually spend a great deal of time trying to push through to get to "greener pastures" on the other side. An insistent tortoise can injure itself by pushing against the chain link and scrapes to its legs and face and even eye injuries are possible. If its vision is blocked by a visual barrier, the tortoise will usually focus on the environment at hand.

Though they love it hot and dry, sulcatas do need some shade and hiding places for resting in the hottest parts of the day. This can be accomplished using shrubs and plants or with man-made structures such as doghouses. Keepers in some areas will be able to get creative and plant fruit trees such as apple, pear, peach, mango, and fig for shade. These trees will not only provide shade, but also will provide tasty treats as the fruit ripens and falls.

Interestingly, captive sulcatas love a water hole to soak in during the heat of summer. You should try to never have standing water in a sulcata pen for any length of time because it can harbor harmful bacteria and it can be a breeding ground for mosquitoes. Also, sulcata skin is very permeable to water and absorbing large amounts of water is unnatural for them. We suggest letting them soak only once a week during summer and once every 2-3 weeks during the cooler months.

The entrance to an African Spurred Tortoise's burrow in Senegal. Photo by Jim Pether.

THE SULCATA BURROW

As mentioned, it is natural behavior for a sulcata tortoise to dig. In the wild, they dig deep burrows. These burrows provide shelter, protection, and some moisture. In captivity, some sulcatas will be enthusiastic diggers and others will not dig, tending to crawl under existing shelters instead. If your sulcata has access to water, shade, and plenty of secure hiding spaces, they will probably not dig. However, some individuals will be diggers and they will be difficult to dissuade. The problem with digging, other than wrecking your yard, is that sulcatas with burrows can occasionally crawl deep into their long burrow on a cold night. If they are not retrievable, they could get chilled, which can lead to respiratory problems, pneumonia, and even death.

WINTER QUARTERS

In moderately warm areas (winters down to 45° F), keepers and breeders typically add doghouses modified to hold heat into their outdoor sulcata pens. A fixture with an incandescent bulb is placed inside or a "pig blanket" is placed underneath the doghouse to add warmth on cold nights. The goal is to keep the tortoises in the 60° to 65° F range. Tortoises will typically come

out during the sunny days, even when it is cool (50° to 55° F), and retreat to the warmth of their shelter in the early evening. In this situation, keepers must check on their tortoises during cold nights to make sure they get inside okay.

In regions with cold winters (below 45° F), your sulcatas will need to be brought indoors to prevent cold-related problems such as respiratory infections and pneumonia.

Two large sulcatas enter their outbuilding as evening approaches.

Many keepers choose to keep stock tanks inside in a special warm room and carry their tortoises inside each evening. The large scale tortoise keepers usually have insulated buildings or greenhouses constructed to keep their tortoises warm during winter. These buildings or greenhouses can be purchased in kit form from local home improvement centers. Also, the classified ads in the newspaper are a good source for a small building. Look under "Portable Buildings". They can usually be purchased and moved relatively inexpensively.

Stalls or divisions can be added within these buildings to keep the males and females or aggressive individuals separated. Though fighting behavior is usually low during the cool winter, tortoises will occasionally still ram each other and possibly injure one another.

Large sulcatas keep warm under a heat lamp in their winter quarters.

Sulcatas are intelligent and will usually instinctively move into and out of their cool weather buildings. They emerge during a sunny day to feed and when a cold evening arrives, they will usually be where they are supposed to be. If they get under a shrub or tree roots, under a building, or in a burrow when a cold night hits, they can get a chill and leave you battling a respiratory infection all winter. This is a common occurrence in tortoise collections in northern parts of the United States, Canada, and much of Europe. If you find that you need to move a big tortoise inside during cold weather, it can be problematic. You have a couple of choices: First, you may have to carry it. This can be difficult, even for two people, once you have a large specimen weighing 75 to 100 pounds or more. Secondly, you might be able to lure a large *G. sulcata* with its favorite food such as an aromatic fruit like banana or melon or a brightly colored one such as an apple or tomato. (This is not easy when they are cold and sluggish!)

Male sulcatas will often ram each other during courtship and breeding season. Occasionally they will flip each other onto their backs - a potentially serious and deadly situation. Photo by Rusty Mills.

HELPFUL HINTS

CAUTION: Be sure to "baby-proof" your outdoor enclosure. First, look for any items that might cause your tortoise to tumble over onto its back. Tortoises can turn over and if unable to right themselves, they can die very quickly, especially on a hot day. The weight of their internal organs pressing down on their lungs (now on the bottom) can also be a fatal situation. This is an occurrence that is very dangerous and many captive tortoises are lost to this type of accident. Objects that can cause a tortoise to accidentally flip over include stairs, low enclosures, concrete blocks, and even each other. Also, males will occasionally flip each other over when pushing each other around the yard.

Shell damage from ramming can occur in these powerful tortoises. These injuries and the related stress can be fatal. However, once a hierarchy is established, these bouts usually occur only during breeding season. Subordinate males and smaller tortoises are smart and usually know when to avoid larger males and choose to beat a hasty retreat when one wanders near.

Make sure that a tortoise cannot come into contact with pesticides and herbicides through their food or captive environment.

Sulcatas and other tortoises are attracted to colorful fruit and flowers and therefore also to small colorful objects like plastic toys and even plastic bags. They will eat these objects and if not passed in the feces, they can cause veterinary emergencies.

Sulcatas are ravenous feeders on just about any plant material. They use the "eat first and ask questions later" feeding method. They will even eat poisonous plants or plant parts if given the opportunity. Signs of poisoning include lethargy, droopy head, drooling, and bloody or loose stools. Check your tortoise area and consult this list for the most common poisonous plants found in yards.

FURTHER READING:

Barnard, S. M. (1996.) Reptile Keeper's Handbook. Krieger Publishing Co. pp. 167-184.

California Turtle and Tortoise Club Poisonous Plant List.

SOME COMMON POISONOUS PLANTS

Bird of Paradise	Mushrooms (some wild)
Bottlebrush	Oleander
Calla Lilly	Poinsettia
Christmas Cactus	Poison Ivy
Common Privet	Poison Oak
Dieffenbachia	Poison Sumac
Dogwood	Pokeweed
English Ivy	Potato (leaves)
Foxglove	Privet
Hemlock	Rhododendron
Impatiens	Rhubarb
Iris	Sage
Jasmine	Snapdragon
Larkspur	Sweet pea
Lily of the Valley	Tomato (leaves)
Marijuana	Tulip
Milk Weed	Verbena
Mistletoe	Wisteria
Morning Glory	Yew

Who Will Be Man's Best Friend?

Dogs and tortoises do not mix! Although many tortoise keepers keep both as pets, it is really unwise to mix dogs and tortoises. The pattern is quite typical. . . Even after living with them peacefully for a while, curiosity and innate behavior gets the best of the dog and soon you will have problems. Dogs will chew on large tortoises, will kill little ones, and will produce feces that the tortoises will eat. For some reason, sulcatas love to eat dog feces. Many African tortoises will seek out hyena feces in the wild as a source of calcium (the ground up bones in the waste). Perhaps this is what is happening with sulcatas? In any event, it is unnatural and a possible source for parasitic infection for your tortoises. As most dog owners know, dogs commonly harbor at least one or two types of parasitic worms. These worms, when transmitted to an exotic species such as your tortoise, might cause more harm than a typical mild worm infection. At the least, these parasites rob your tortoises of nutrition, strength, energy, and livelihood.

Chapter SEVEN: FEEDING

African Spurred Tortoises eat a lot!   They are browsers who actively munch leaves and trim grass of its nutritious tips. In the wild their diet is high in fiber, low in protein, and very low in fat. This low nutrition diet leads to slow growth and a daily routine spent searching for food and moisture in a very harsh environment.

Unlike this life in nature, captive African Spurred Tortoises are presented with an abundance of food and a veritable smorgasbord by thoughtful keepers. Usually, new owners experiment with a variety of food and both natural and commercial diets are considered. Care must be taken, however, to make sure that tortoises receive a diet that recreates their natural intake of food as closely as possible. For sulcata keepers, the goal is to provide a diet that has lots of fiber, but is low in protein and fat content.

A group of large African Spurred Tortoises enjoying a meal of red peppers, bell peppers, tomatoes, and other fruits and vegetables. Photo by Rusty Mills.

The ideal foods for your African Spurred Tortoise are grasses, prairie hay, clover, dandelions, and a variety of leaves. They also enjoy dark green lettuce, kale, carrot tops, broccoli, squash, and more. In addition to these, your tortoise can feed on flowers (see Poisonous Plant list), alfalfa hay (modest amounts as it is high in protein and calcium), and a variety of other plant material. Spineless *Opuntia* cactus pads are a very good food for all tortoises (Check the vegetable section of your local grocery that offers a variety of Hispanic foods).

We add a sprinkle of multivitamin powder and calcium with Vitamin D3 onto our tortoises' salads every 5-6 feedings. For growing babies and reproductive females, we add the calcium-vitamin mixture every 2-3 feedings.

Great Supplemental Foods for your Sulcata Tortoise

Romaine lettuce
Red leaf lettuce
Green leaf lettuce
Collard greens
Kale
Carrot tops and carrots
Squash
Red cabbage
Sweet potatoes
Pumpkin
Melons *
Cantaloupe *
Banana *
Apples *
Pears *
Clover
Geraniums
Hibiscus
Nasturtium
Rose

* Feed fruit to *G. sulcata* only sparingly because of the high sugar content.

Become a Gardener

Plant a vegetable garden near your tortoise enclosure. It will be a healthy and enjoyable hobby and will help cut your vegetable bill at the grocery store. Be sure to use a raised bed, if it is kept in the same area as your tortoises, made with landscape timbers or railroad ties if it is kept in the same area as your tortoises. Plant squash, zucchini, varieties of lettuce, kale, broccoli, melons, and those veggies that your tortoises are especially fond of.

In the wild, an African Spurred Tortoise's diet consists of high fiber and roughly 5% protein and 2% fat. General commercial tortoise foods – pellets, sticks, and biscuits – do not recreate the natural requirements for these tortoises.

Nutritional Analysis of Some Commercially Available Diets

MAZURI Tortoise Diet®
Protein – not less than 15.0%
Fat – not less than 3.0%
Fiber – not more than 18.0%

ZOOMED Box Turtle and Land Tortoise Food®
Protein – max. 18.4%
Fat – min. 5.2%
Fiber – max. 10.0%

Flukers Tortoise Diet®
Protein – not less than 15.0%
Fat – not less than 3.0%
Fiber – not more than 18.0%

Pretty Pets Tortoise Food®
Protein – 8.0%
Fat – 3.0%
Fiber – 13.0%

Rep-Cal Tortoise Food®
Protein – 19.0%
Fat – 1.0%
Fiber – 18.0%

Most of these commercial foods are more suited to Red-footed Tortoises, Yellow-footed Tortoises, and Hinge-backed Tortoises as these species normally take in larger amounts of protein through eating carrion and invertebrates in the wild. These commercial feeds should be used sparingly or only as a very small part of your African Spurred Tortoise's diet.

WATER
It should be abundantly obvious by now that African Spurred Tortoises love it hot and dry! Their natural habitat with its arid, sandy soil with few shrubs and dry grasses sees very little water.

Three young African Spurred Tortoises soaking in a bath of shallow, purified water. Photo by Rusty Mills.

Interestingly, in captivity these tortoises seem to be attracted to water and will spend a lot of time soaking in pools of rainwater or areas where a garden hose has been left running.

It is a good idea to limit the amount of soaking they do and we feel that it is never a good idea to leave pools of standing water in an outdoor sulcata enclosure. These pools can be breeding grounds for bacteria and mosquitoes. Instead, find a very large flat dish like those used under flower pots. Keep fresh water available for them in these dishes. They are also easy to clean and sterilize. We clean them once a week (or when needed) with a light bleach solution and let them air dry in the sun when possible.

When they are small, soak young tortoises in a flat dish of purified room temperature water. We suggest soaking babies and juveniles once a week especially in the summer and we offer the large tortoises additional water once every ten days to two weeks during the hottest part of the year. Be careful that the water level is only up to a point just above the edge of the plastron (covering the legs). We suggest soaking them once a week. Soak them for just a few minutes while you clean the cage or remove feces or leftover greens from their enclosure.

Chapter EIGHT: HEALTH

Captive African Spurred Tortoises are very hardy and tolerant of a wide range of captive conditions. However, occasional accidents or lapses in good husbandry produce a tortoise with an ailment or injury. Watch for respiratory distress, weight loss, runny stools, and physical changes. These are all signs of a problem.

If a tortoise is alert and feeding, it is fairly easy for a keeper to treat minor problems. If a tortoise is lethargic and refusing to

eat or is suffering from a more serious problem or injury, call your veterinarian. Find a veterinarian with reptile (turtle and tortoise) experience first by visiting a local herp society meeting or by calling the vets in your area and inquiring about their reptile experience and especially experience with tortoises. (Most veterinarians will have limited experience, but more and more are becoming familiar with reptile care.) The Association of Reptile and Amphibian Veterinarians (A.R.A.V.) is an organization of veterinarians that specialize in reptile and amphibian care. You can access their website at www.arav.com to find a qualified veterinarian in your area.

RESPIRATORY AILMENTS

Respiratory problems occur when a tortoise gets chilled or is kept in sub-optimal conditions. Minor problems can be corrected with heat and a drop in humidity. If not corrected, minor problems can progress to more serious conditions such as pneumonia. Signs of a respiratory problem include labored breathing, a nasal discharge, a gaping mouth, puffy eyes, lethargy, and a loss of appetite.

To correct minor respiratory problems, increase the warmth of the enclosure with an extra heat source such as a fixture with an incandescent bulb and/or a heating pad under the enclosure. Keep the enclosure hot and dry. Bump up the temperature from 80° to 90° (27° to 32° C) and increase the hot spot from 95° to 100° F (32° to 38° C) range.

More severe cases or those that do not respond to added heat will require a course of antibiotics. We have found Baytril® (Enrofloxacin) and Garamycin® (Gentomycin) to be effective for treating respiratory ailments in turtles and tortoises. (You will need to consult a veterinarian for treatment or to obtain antibiotic drugs.)

INJURIES

Injuries occur in these active tortoises. As mentioned earlier, the males have a tendency to ram each other (and other tortoises), especially during the breeding season and throughout the

Antibiotic Dosages

Baytril® (Enrofloxacin) - **5** mg./kg subcutaneous, intramuscular, or oral daily for a week. *(Ed. Note: We have had good success with adding the proper dosage onto a piece of banana or favorite food.)*

Genticin® (Gentomicin) – **5** mg./kg intramuscular every **72** hours for **7-14** days. Hydration.

Amikin® (Amikacin) - **5-10** mg./kg intramuscular every **48** hours for **7-14** days. Hydration and warm environment.

From *Veterinary Management of Tortoises and Turtles* by Stuart McArthur (1996) Blackwell Science Limited.

year as they establish a hierarchy. This aggressive behavior can lead to limb and shell injuries. Also, accidents occasionally occur when tortoises push against fences, topple over when climbing, turn each other over, etc.

A wash of Betadine® works well to promote the healing of minor shell scrapes and injuries and kills off harmful bacteria. Be careful using Betadine® on an open wound. (The iodine solution kills much of the healthy skin that should grow and pull the wound back together.) Instead, we use sterile water to clean the wound and use an antibiotic lotion, or Silvadene® ointment to prevent bacteria growth in and around the wound.

Serious injuries will usually involve a visit to your vet as they might require stitches, gauze wraps, or even a fiberglass patch for severe shell damage.

PARASITES
EXTERNAL PARASITES

Many wild-caught tortoises have been imported with ticks. If you find a tick on your tortoise, it should be removed right away. Ticks drain your tortoise of blood and energy, transmit diseases, and can multiply by the hundreds. To remove the tick, grasp it firmly as close to the point of attachment to the tortoise as possible, and pull it out. Avoid leaving the head of the tick imbedded in the tortoise's skin. (This rarely occurs.) There are special tick-removing tweezers available from most camping and outdoor supply stores. Place a dab of antibiotic lotion on the area where the tick was removed for a few days afterwards.

AFRICAN HEARTWATER DISEASE

Importation and movement of *Geochelone sulcata*, *G. pardalis* (Leopard Tortoise), and *Kinixys belliana* (Hinge-backed Tortoise) have been banned since March 2000 when shipments

The African Hinge-backed Tortoise, Kinixys belliana is one of the tortoises that had travel restrictions placed upon it due to the African Heartwater disease scare of 2000.

from Africa were discovered that contained a sinister tropical tick. The tick (*Amblyomma* species) typically carries a parasitic microbe (*Cowdria* species). This microbe is known to kill ruminants such as antelopes and water buffalo by causing their pericardium (the membrane around the heart) to fill with fluid. This microbe is only moderately dangerous in Africa but the USDA felt that it could be transmitted to hoofstock in the United States and could wipe out huge numbers of cows, sheep, goats, and deer if it were to become established. Of special concern was Florida, a tropical environment known to be especially favorable for sustaining exotic species that have escaped into the wild. The USDA passed a rule immediately restricting the transport of these three species of tortoises. Now, documents from a veterinarian are required for their transport. These documents must certify that the tortoises are free of ticks.

INTERNAL PARASITES

Imported tortoises, or those mixed with imported specimens, are often plagued by a variety of internal parasites. You can verify an infestation if you see worms or proglottids (worm segments) in a tortoise's feces or by having a fecal check done by your veterinarian. Adult parasitic worms pass many eggs out with a tortoise's feces. These eggs can be seen under a microscope.

PANACUR® (Fenbendazole)
Panacur® is recommended for the elimination of parasitic worms.

DOSAGE OF PANACUR®
    25-50 mg. / kg.
    2 ml / kg (2.5%)
    (1 kg = 2.2 pounds)

Dosage from *Understanding Reptile Parasites* by Roger Klingenberg DVM, (1993) Advanced Vivarium Systems, Inc. Mission Viejo, California, USA.

We use Panacur® (Fenbendazole) and Flagyl® (Metronidazole) to eliminate most parasitic infections. Panacur® works well for roundworms (nematodes) and Flagyl® works well for eliminating amoebic organisms.

TTPG Hint: The easiest way to deparasitize most chelonians with Panacur® is to plaster their favorite food with it. A piece of banana or mango can be covered with the proper dosage of Panacur® and carefully fed to the tortoise. In a community situation, be sure that each individual tortoise receives a "dosed up" piece of banana or other fruit and that an eager individual doesn't snatch the food from its fellow tortoises. Watch closely and keep a *Tortoise Notebook* handy for jotting down information that you won't remember later. In addition, when we see a tortoise "eat" a dose of Panacur®, we dab a small splotch of acrylic paint onto its carapace. This small splotch is color-coded for 1st treatment (yellow), 2nd treatment (red), etc. In the *Tortoise Notebook* we note the date, time, food accepted, estimated dosage, tortoise's name or id number, sex of tortoise, etc. After 3-4 treatments, the infected tortoise's fecal sample is rechecked for presence of parasites or their ova. The vet's printout is added to this tortoise's page in the *Tortoise Notebook*.

We suggest that each of your tortoises that lives outdoors, even those that are captive-hatched, be tested for parasites once a year. Simply bottle up a small fecal sample, note which tortoise "deposited it" in your *Tortoise Notebook*, and take it to your local

---

IVERMECTIN®

Do not use Ivermectin® on tortoises. Ivermectin® is commonly available at vet supply companies and at feed stores. Ivermectin® will remove parasites from horses efficiently but it will kill your tortoises very quickly. Do not use it.

FLAGYL® (Metronidazole)

Flagyl® is recommended for the elimination of amoebic parasites and gram-negative bacterial organisms.

Flagyl® is available as a liquid and as a 250 mg. tablet or a 500 mg. tablet.

DOSAGE OF FLAGYL®
25-50 mg. / kg
3 ml / kg (2.3%)
(1 kg = 2.2 pounds)

Dosage from *Understanding Reptile Parasites* by Roger Klingenberg DVM, (1993) Advanced Vivarium Systems, Inc. Mission Viejo, California, USA.

veterinarian for a check. Don't put the sample in alcohol or other preservative; keeping it dry or in water is best.

Become knowledgeable about parasites, especially parasitic worms. Use good husbandry and hygiene to avoid infection and reinfection. Look for potential problems and stop them before they cause you heartache.

Other Health Issues

PYRAMIDING

Pyramiding is when a tortoise shows abnormal growth on its carapace, making it look bumpy. This condition is caused when a tortoise eats a diet that is too high in protein and too low in calcium. It is seen in captive sulcatas when a tortoise is fed solely on commercial diets or even when a tortoise eats too much of a good diet.

There is some disagreement on the damaging effects of pyramiding . . . but not too much disagreement. Some keepers say that pyramiding is simply the sign of a healthy, well-fed cap-

Pyramiding in a three-year old G. sulcata. *Photo by Rusty Mills.*

tive tortoise. Most breeders (including us) however, believe that pyramiding is aberrant and is characteristic of unnatural growth. No long-term studies have been completed, but it is well documented that captive tortoises that have unnatural growth and especially those that are obese, exhibit kidney and liver problems that significantly shorten their lives.

IRREGULAR SCUTES

Occasionally, young sulcatas are seen with irregular scutes. This abnormality can range from barely noticeable to quite severe. These "spiderweb" scutes are caused when an egg has been incubated too hot either accidentally or by a breeder trying to rush the incubation time. Though unnatural-looking, these tortoises usually do not exhibit other health problems.

LUMPY JAWS

A sulcata's jaw should be strong, solid, and symmetrical. There should be no bumps and no overgrowth of the beak. Both are signs of poor nutrition or a poor captive environment.

SOFT SHELL

Soft shell is a more severe malady arising from lack of direct sunlight and calcium. This happens when a tortoise's blood stream shaves calcium from its bones and its shell to meet the calcium needs of the muscular and other body systems, leaving the tortoise's shell soft and pliable. This condition can be corrected by the addition of calcium and vitamin supplements on its food and by the addition of plenty of natural sunlight.

Most health-related problems can be prevented or resolved quickly if your tortoises are kept hot and dry in a proper captive environment. Be sure to offer them plenty of grass for food and occasionally add high-quality calcium and vitamins to a mixed, finely chopped salad. Offer a proper substrate and keep their enclosure clean.

Chapter NINE: BREEDING

In captivity, African Spurred Tortoises are very pro-
lific. In nature, a female typically lays only one clutch of
eggs per year. The hatching of this nest coincides with the
onset of the rainy season and the resulting growth of plants
for the hatchlings. In captivity, a large well-fed female can
lay multiple clutches of from 10 to 20 eggs each year. Fertility is usually high and a sulcata breeder can find himself
or herself with lots of healthy babies each year. If an "out-
let" is developed, the babies can be sold quite easily. The
money raised from this tortoise breeding operation purchase
other tortoises.

*A pair of large adult African Spurred Tortoises mating. The female will typically eat
and pay little attention to the male during this time. Photo by Rusty Mills.*

The dilemma then arises . . . Are there too many African Spurred Tortoises around? Like pythons and other oversized pet reptiles, we often ask ourselves, 'Are these wonderful animals becoming disposable pets once they get too big? When they get big will people dump them?' The question is being answered now and unfortunately that is what is happening. There are even reports of African Spurred Tortoises being turned loose into desert tortoise habitat in the fragile deserts of southern California and Arizona. Please do not ever release an animal into the wild. There are potential dangers to native wildlife including disease transmission, competition for food and habitat, and other damage that is poorly understood. Be a conscientious breeder. Enjoy your tortoises and don't feel pressed to breed them and produce lots of babies. Be mindful that breeding tortoises at a young age can also be unhealthy for them.

A comparison of two large African Spurred Tortoises. The male (left) has a wider flattened anal notch, longer tail, and a noticeable concavity to his plastron while the female (right) has a rounded anal notch and shorter tail. Photo by Rusty Mills.

SEXING

Though it is difficult to determine visually in a young tortoise, at about 12" to 14" (typically 3-4 years) your sulcata will begin showing some signs of its sex. At this size it is usually 6" to 8" (2-3 years) away from breeding, but you will have an idea of what the sex of your tortoise is and your ability to produce baby sulcatas in the future.

FEMALES

Females usually mature at 17" to 18" which usually translates to 7 to 8 years of healthy growth in captivity. Female sulcatas have a short tail. The shape of the anal notch is comparatively wide and rounded to allow the passage of eggs. Photo by Rusty Mills.

MALES

Females usually reach sexual maturity at 17" to 18;" Male sulcatas usually mature at 15" to 16" which is usually indicative of 5 to 6 years of healthy growth in captivity. Male sulcatas have a longer tail that usually folds to the side. The opening of the anal notch is quite wide. Male African Spurred Tortoises, like other male tortoises, have a fairly deep concavity to the plastron. Photo by Rusty Mills.

Courtship and Pre-mating Behavior

AGGRESSION

Aggression exhibited by male African Spurred Tortoises during the breeding season is common and occasionally violent. As they mature, males will begin ramming and mounting other males to assert their dominance. During the breeding time, overly aggressive males will occasionally attack other tortoises, pets, and even people, ramming them with their gular projections with incredible force.

Female sulcatas sometimes exhibit aggressive behaviors as well. They will shove males to prevent unwanted advances and will often ram other tortoises that come too close to their "secure" resting space. This is common when the females are gravid (have eggs) and especially when egg-laying is imminent.

MATING

The large male sulcata mounts the female with little or no courtship behavior other than "the chase". A successful breeding

A male sulcata uses his weight to immobilize the female during copulation. Photo by Rusty Mills.

male typically outweighs the female by many, many pounds. The extreme size discrepancy allows the male to weigh down the female and immobilize her. This mating practice is also seen in Galapagos Tortoises and Aldabra Tortoises. Smaller male sulcatas are usually unsuccessful in breeding as they are dislodged, pushed away, or carried off by a larger female. During copulation, the male will usually raise and lower himself, scraping the female's carapace. There is also usually some tail stimulation and vocalization during mating.

VOCALIZATION

While mating, male sulcatas often emit a loud quacking sound. This vocalization is common in a variety of the world's tortoises from small to large.

EGG-LAYING

In the wild, most breeding and egg-laying revolves around the rainy season (when it exists). Typically, a female will lay a single clutch of eggs just before the rainy season. The eggs incubate for around 200 days and the hatchlings emerge just before the next rainy season. This "system" allows the young tortoises to take advantage of the new and abundant plant growth. In captivity, mating activity for African Spurred Tortoises can begin in cooler months as spring approaches and typically lasts throughout the warmer months.

A female African Spurred Tortoise laying her eggs in her native habitat in Senegal. Photo by Jim Pether.

Within about 30 days of mating, the female will begin showing signs of imminent egg-laying. As this time approaches, the female begins to eat less and becomes restless, pacing the enclosure. Over a period of 5-

10 days she may dig as many as 3-4 test holes. When ready to lay eggs, she will dig the actual nest, which is usually a long and arduous feat. She will dig with both front and back legs, excavating a 24" diameter hole that is roughly 12" deep. Within this hole, she will dig a smaller (8" diameter by 10" deep) inner hole for the egg chamber. If the ground is hard, she will urinate as she digs to soften the earth. After digging and laying from 10 to 20 eggs inside, she will take 1-2 hours to cover the nest. She will cover the nest efficiently and hide it well, so be diligent and watch for digging activity so you don't lose the opportunity to remove and incubate the eggs. Removal of the eggs is best done in the first few days to prevent injury to the developing embryos.

Small female sulcatas will typically lay smaller clutches of only 10 to 12 eggs. A larger female will usually lay 20 to 25 eggs. In areas with warm springs and summers, sulcatas can lay three or four clutches every 30 to 50 days. In hotter environments, a well-fed female sulcata can lay as many as six clutches of eggs each year. Often, the first clutch will have a lower fertility rate than later clutches.

Chapter TEN: THE EGGS AND INCUBATION

THE EGGS

Healthy sulcata eggs are round with fairly brittle shells and are usually in the 1.5" to 2" and 25 to 30 gram range depending on the individual female tortoise.

Once you've discovered the eggs and removed them from the nest, you have a couple of options. You can

A clutch of newly laid African Spurred Tortoise eggs. Photo by Rusty Mills.

keep it simple and incubate the eggs in a plastic shoe box in a dark, warm area such as a closet or you can place them in a commercial or homemade incubator.

Sulcata eggs typically do not go through a diapause, but they have an interesting habit of hatching over an extended period of time. Eggs from a single clutch laid within a few minutes of each other can hatch over a two-week period.

DIGGING THE EGGS

The newly laid eggs can be carefully dug up with your hands or a small shovel. As you reach the eggs in the nest, carefully brush away the substrate and remove the eggs one by one. As you gently remove them, mark the top of each egg with an X in pencil as you move them to the container in which they will be incubated. This will let you know the position that they were laid to prevent rolling and to show you the position in which they should be incubated. As an incubation substrate for sulcata eggs, we use a mixture of ∫ dampened sand and ˘ peat moss. We use the sand-peat mixture for a couple of reasons: 1. This is a

---

"natural" mix 2. We have found that most turtle eggs incubated in this sand-peat mixture have a higher rate of hatching. It appears that the acidity of the peat slowly erodes the surface of the eggs as they incubate and this allows easier "pipping" (emergence) by the hatchlings. This mixture is initially dampened with purified or distilled water to the point that it clumps but does not drip water out of a tightly squeezed handful. Make sure there is no excess water in the bottom of the container. Make a depression with your thumb or a spoon in the damp substrate and gently place the egg into the depression. Carefully push the substrate up around the egg, leaving only the top slightly exposed. After all of the eggs have been removed, we cover the eggs with a layer of very lightly dampened sand or vermiculite to hold in the moisture.

TEMPERATURE, HUMIDITY, AND TIME FOR INCUBATION

Sulcata eggs, like sulcata tortoises, are very forgiving. We recommend an incubation temperature of 86° F (30° C) and 75% to 85% humidity. At this temperature the tortoises will begin hatching in roughly 90 days but hatching can take place in the following week or two.

Lower temperatures will extend the time and hotter temperatures can speed up the hatching by a week or even two.

We recommend that you don't exceed

TEMPERATURE-DEPENDENT SEXUAL DETERMINATION (TSD)

It has been widely known from recent research that many species of turtles and tortoises exhibit TSD. In these species, the sex of the emerging babies has a direct connection to the temperature at which the eggs were incubated. Typically, eggs incubated at low temperatures produce males, eggs incubated at high temperatures produce females, and those incubated mid-range produce a mix of both males and females.

Little research has been completed, but it is apparent from conversations with private breeders across the country that the sex of *Geochelone sulcata* hatchlings is influenced by the temperature at which they were incubated.

80° F (27° C) on the low end and 88° F (31° C) on the high end. Be observant - Eggs incubated too cold will fail to develop and those incubated too hot may kill the developing the embryos.

SHELF METHOD

Eggs can be incubated on a shelf in a dark closet. They should be watched closely to monitor humidity and temperature. They should be warm as eggs incubated too cool will not develop. When incubated in this manner, eggs will typically take longer to hatch, as it will no doubt be cooler than in an incubator. On a shelf system, you usually remove the possibility of eggs overheating – an occasional occurrence when using an electric incubator. Also, some breeders feel that the natural daily fluctuation of temperatures in this shelf system gives them more vigorous and healthy hatchlings.

INCUBATORS

There are a variety of incubators on the market. They can be purchased from farm and garden stores and on the Internet. We have found that Hovabator® incubators are inexpensive and work well. Make sure to set up the incubator for a few days to make sure that the proper temperature is established before the eggs are placed inside. Take the shoe boxes containing the eggs and place them inside the incubator. Make careful notes in your Tortoise Notebook. Include the date the eggs were laid, the temperature and the humidity inside the incubator, dates eggs hatched, etc.

We add a Radio Shack® thermo - hygro temperature/

This hand-made incubator has been in use for ten years and has successfully hatched hundreds of sulcata eggs. Photo by Rusty Mills.

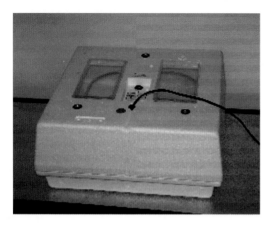

Hovabator® incubators are inexpensive and are in use by reptile

humidity gauge in the top of each incubation container. This allows us to monitor the proper incubation temperature and humidity and lets us keep notes of the daily temperature and humidity. These notes can be useful when your tortoise lays again. Also it lets you share with other tortoise breeders the conditions which were successful and those which were not successful.

GOOD EGGS AND BAD EGGS

As the tortoise embryo develops within the egg, a number of changes occur. In most tortoise eggs, there is a noticeable change in the external appearance of the egg. The egg typically darkens and loses the pinkish tint seen in a newly laid egg. "Chalking" is the appearance of a white opacity to the developing egg. This can appear as a band around the middle of the egg, chalkiness at the ends of the eggs, or an overall change from pinkish or yellowish to white. This "chalking" occurs when the calcium moves from the egg's shell to the developing embryo within. This is a sign that the egg is fertile and that the embryo is developing.

If an egg shows no darkening or change in color, it is most likely infertile. However, you should never discard eggs as even eggs that have discolored, become dented, and even those that have small cracks or slight damage have produced healthy baby turtles.

As the end of the incubation period for a particular species nears, carbon dioxide builds up within the egg and the young turtle is forced out of the egg and pipping, the first stage of hatching occurs.

PIPPING AND THE "EGG TOOTH"

Hatching occurs when the baby tortoise cuts or "pecks" its way out of the egg. This process is aided by the presence of a caruncle or "egg tooth" on the tip of its snout. This structure varies from species to species, but is typically a small, hard projection. The baby African Spurred Tortoise forces a hole or slice in the egg with the "egg tooth" and then the baby tortoise will use his legs, head, or mouth to widen the opening in the egg. Once it is able to breathe the outside air, it may rest within the egg for an hour up to several days, gaining strength, absorbing the remainder of the yolk sac, and preparing for the struggles that lay ahead. Within a few days of emerging from the egg, the "egg tooth" falls off.

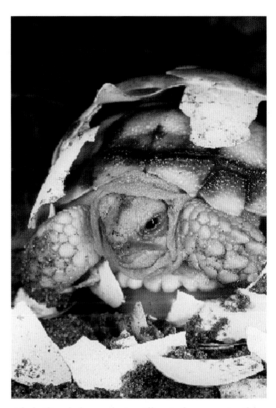

A baby Geochelone sulcata *will rest after emerging from the egg. The yolk sac of this baby can be clearly seen. Photo by Bill Love.*

Be patient. Babies can hatch up to 14 days later from the same clutch of eggs.

Upon hatching, make sure the baby tortoise's yolk sac has been completely absorbed. If the yolk sac is abnormally large, you have a couple of choices:

1. You can leave the tortoise in the warmth of the incubator. In a couple of days, the sac should be completely absorbed. In some areas, small "carrion" flies or gnats will invade an incubator, drawn by the albumen and other tissue in the newly vacated eggs. The larvae of these flies will attack recently hatched babies and can kill them within a matter of hours. If you feel that the incubator is unsafe during this time and your hatchlings need further absorption of their yolk sac, you can remove the empty eggs and replace the substrate with new, clean substrate.

2. Another choice is to move the hatchlings into a small plastic tub or shoe box with a clean, damp paper towel in the bottom. Let them rest quietly in the safety and warmth of the tub. In a couple of days, the sac should be absorbed completely. If they come out with the yolk sac absorbed, and only a small button showing, set them up in their first home.

Chapter ELEVEN: HATCHLINGS

Sometimes it is hard to realize that the small G. sulcata hatchling will grow into one of the world's largest tortoises.

Hatchling sulcatas emerge from the egg at about 2°" long and weighing a little over an ounce (28 to 32 grams). They emerge from the egg a little folded up, but seem to inflate into a normal appearing hatchling within a day or two of hatching. They have a pale yellow carapace with dark brown seams. Within a few days to as much as a week, they begin the mission of eating, exploring, and growing. They are typically active during feeding time and spend much of the day resting near the hot spot in their enclosure.

A BABY SULCATA'S FIRST HOME

The first enclosure for a small tortoise can be a terrarium in the 10 to 20 gallon range. We have found 20-gallon long aquariums to be ideal. The length of these aquariums (30" x 12" x 12") gives you a good space to establish a temperature gradient within the enclosure. By placing a clamp type fixture with a 100 watt (spot) T-Rex Active UV-heat bulb® over one end, the keeper can establish the required 90° to 95° F (32° to 35° C) basking spot and UV rays that are essential for these growing babies. Maintain the other end in the 80° to 85° F (27° to 29° C) range.

TUBS

If you hatch out many babies, you may choose to raise them in small cement-mixing tubs. These tubs are inexpensive and make good enclosures for small tortoises. They can be stacked on a rack system, allowing you to keep many tortoises in a relatively small space.

SUBSTRATE

For large numbers of baby sulcatas, you will probably want to use rabbit food as a substrate as it is safe, easy to clean, and is inexpensive. Paper towels are also good because they are inexpensive. When the towel gets soiled, it can be easily removed and replaced with new. A sand and peat mixture is an inexpensive and natural substrate. Add rocks, wood, and plants to make an interesting and exciting tortoise enclosure.

HEAT

As mentioned above, high heat and aridity with a temperature gradient is necessary to keep these tortoises healthy. We maintain our babies in an enclosure that stays 80° to 85° F (27° to 29° C) around the clock and that has a basking spot that stays at 95° F (35° C) during the day. During the winter we add a heating pad on the low setting underneath the "hot" end of their vivarium to maintain the proper temperature.

LIGHTING

We use shop light fixtures with high-quality UVB bulbs and a T-REX Active UV-Heat ® bulb above all of our indoor turtles and tortoises.

SHELTER

Add cork bark, drift wood, or a commercial shelter.

FIRST FOODS

First foods for a hatchling sulcata should include grass, dandelions, clover, and a finely chopped salad consisting of a variety of leafy plants including kale, romaine lettuce, redleaf lettuce, greenleaf lettuce, cabbage, zucchini, broccoli, alfalfa, and others.

Shelters for your small tortoises can be as creative as you can find. This handmade ceramic shelter works well and is esthetically pleasing.

Remember, LOW PROTEIN is the goal. You want to maintain variety and prevent pyramiding and obesity.

For a finicky baby, offer strawberry, red bell pepper, or bananas. These seem to stimulate non-feeding tortoises with their color or smell. Once feeding, switch any finicky eaters to the recommended healthy diet.

OUTDOORS

As much as possible, place your baby sulcatas outside to reap the benefits of direct sunlight. Obviously, for small sulcatas, extreme care must be taken that the outdoor enclosure is secure. In some areas, a secure top will be necessary. Add some shelter and shady spots inside the enclosure.

This secure top will help avoid predation by dogs, cats, raccoons, opossums, rats, and birds. (All of these are known predators of baby tortoises.) You can avoid most problems by adding a secure cover made of wood and sturdy hardware cloth. This cover will keep all but the smallest predators out and allow helpful UVB rays in.

Baby sulcatas typically feed better outside and as they roam their enclosure, they have access to additional food items.

A beautiful and functional outdoor pen for young African Spurred Tortoises.

Baby sulcatas show their distinctive personalities almost immediately. They are alert, inquisitive, and extremely docile. They will eagerly eat small pieces of greens from their keeper's hands and roam out to investigate when you come near them. Within a very short time they will transform themselves from newly hatched tortoises into a member of the family.

THE FUTURE

From their first appearance in captivity, African Spurred Tortoises captured the hearts of tortoise keepers. These giants with their beautiful sandy tan color, intelligent eyes, and inquisitive personality were immediately a big hit!

Despite the fascination, some keepers discovered right away that African Spurred Tortoises were too much for them to handle. These tortoises get too big for most people. For others, these tortoises were worth modifying their yards, enlarging their grocery bills, and changing their daily routines.

Those just beginning to keep tortoises have to discover if sulcatas are right for them. The situation is very similar to hobbyists who consider large pythons, giant lizards, and venomous snakes. They can be advised and informed and despite a wealth of information from books, articles, and websites, they have to find out for themselves if these tortoises are right for them.

Please do not dump unwanted tortoises. If you decide to move your tortoise on to another situation, take a little time to find a legitimate adoption organization for turtles and tortoises, especially large tortoises. Find organizations such as the Turtle and Tortoise Preservation Group and Turtle Homes that specialize in large, naturalistic environ-

ments for their animals and that have a network of keepers and breeders with which to place tortoises. We encourage you to join a local turtle and tortoise club or herpetological society. Read, explore, and visit with keepers and breeders in your area to find out what works best.

We hope that through this book you will understand a little more about your tortoise and be able to give it a wonderful captive environment. This environment can revolve around proper care and a daily life that keeps the tortoise both healthy and stimulated. Keep in mind that in today's world with its emphasis on technology, expansion, and fast-paced routines, these tortoises slow us down and keep us connected to the natural world.

Thank you.

RUSS GURLEY

Director,
Turtle and Tortoise Preservation Group

BIBLIOGRAPHY

Proceedings: Conservation, Restoration, and Management of Tortoises and Turtles – An International Conference. (1997) New York Turtle and Tortoise Society.

Bartlett, R. D. and Bartlett, P. (1996) Turtles and Tortoises: A Complete Pet Owner's Manual. Barron's Educational Series, Inc. Hauppauge, N.Y.

Bull, J. J. and Vogt, R. C. (1979) Temperature-Dependent Sex Determination in Turtles. Science 206:1186-1188.

Ernst, C.H. and Barbour, R.W. (1989) Turtles of the World. Smithsonian Institution Press.

Flower, S.S. (1928) Examination of a living specimen of the great African tortoise, (Testudo sulcata). Proceedings of the Zoological Society of London. 1928:654.

Highfield, A. (1996) Practical Encyclopedia of Keeping and Breeding Tortoises and Freshwater Tortoises. Carapace Press. England.

Highfield, A. (2002) Understanding Reptile Lighting Systems. Tortoise Trust Web site - www.tortoisetrust.org/articles/lighting.html

Jamison, B and Jamison, B. (1993) Bob and Judy Thomas Interview, Tortuga Gazette April 1993. 29(4): 4-5.

Kaplan, M. (1996) Sulcata Tortoises - African Spurred Tortoises, Geochelone sulcata. www.anapsid.org;sulcata.html.

Klingenberg, R. (1993) Understanding Reptile Parasites, Advanced Vivarium Systems, California.

McArthur, S. (1996) Veterinary Management of Tortoises and Turtles. Blackwell Science, Limited. England.

Paull, R.C. (1997) Great African Spur-thighed or Sulcata Tortoise Geochelone sulcata. Green Nature Books, Homestead, Florida.

Pritchard, P.C.H. (1979) Encyclopedia of Turtles. T.F.H. Publications, Inc. New Jersey, 895 pp.

Stearns, B. C. (1988) Captive husbandry and propagation of the African Spurred Tortoise, Geochelone sulcata. Proceedings, International Herpetology Symposium, San Antonio, Texas. 566 pp.

Vosjoli, P. de (1996) The General Care and Maintenance of Popular Tortoises. Advanced Vivarium Systems, California.

Wilson, R. and Wilson, R. (1997) The Care and Breeding of the African Spurred Tortoise Geochelone sulcata. Carapace Press, England.

PHOTO GALLERY

An unusual caramel-colored African Spurred Tortoise. Photo by Jim Pether.

A large African Spurred Tortoise rests at the entrance to its burrow in the Tortoise Village near Sangalkam, Senegal. Photo by Jim Pether.

A comparison of the plastrons of two large adult Geochelone sulcata *tortoises. The female (left) has gular projections that are smaller, thinner and less flared than those of the male (right). Photo by Rusty Mills.*

A posterior view shows the male's sloping back marginals and the widened, flattened anal notch. The female's anal notch (right) is rounded, allowing easier passage of the eggs. Photo by Rusty Mills.

About the only courtship behavior seen in this species is an incessant chasing and nudging during the warmer months. Once caught, the female will be mounted and copulation will last from 30 minutes to an hour. Photo by Rusty Mills.

Two female African Spurred Tortoises digging nests in the Tortoise Village near Sangalkam, Senegal. Photo by Jim Pether.

The African Spurred Tortoise

A hatchling albino African Spurred Tortoise and its normal appearing sibling, hatched in 2002. Photo courtesy Ben Siegel Reptiles.

A large Geochelone sulcata *retreating to its burrow in the early evening. This photo was taken at the Tortoise Village near Sangalkam, Senegal. Photo by Jim Pether.*